NATIONAL GEOGRAPHIC **OUR WORLD**

Sweet Surprises
Accidental Food Inventions

by Jennifer Monaghan

NATIONAL GEOGRAPHIC LEARNING

CENGAGE Learning

Some inventions are created on purpose. Their inventors work hard to create them. The light bulb, the television, and the car are examples of these kinds of inventions.

But some inventions are created by accident. Their inventors don't know they are creating something until they see the invention. Some popular snacks and desserts were invented this way.

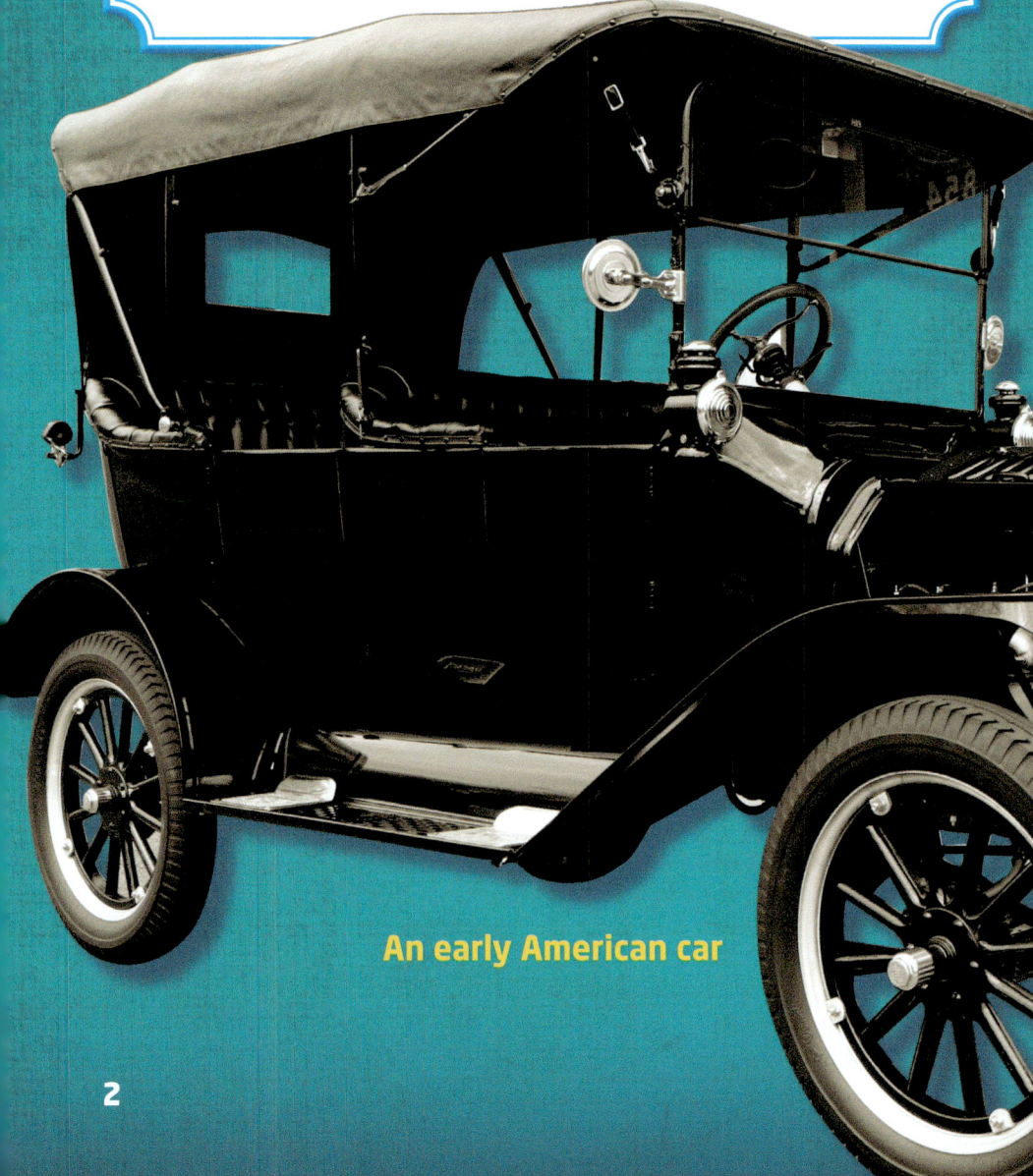

An early American car

An early television

An early light bulb

Chocolate Chip Cookies

In 1930, a woman named Ruth Wakefield owned a small hotel in the United States with her husband. Ruth used to bake chocolate cookies for the guests. But one day, Ruth had a problem. She didn't have any chocolate powder for her cookies.

Ruth came up with a solution. She broke a bar of chocolate into many small pieces. Then she put the chocolate pieces into the cookie dough.

Ruth expected the pieces of chocolate to melt and make the cookies all chocolate. But the pieces didn't melt. Instead of making chocolate cookies, she made chocolate chip cookies!

Ruth agreed to let a chocolate company put her recipe on the packages of their chocolate. In return, the company gave her free chocolate chips for life.

Ruth Wakefield

Today, the chocolate chip cookie is America's favorite cookie!

5

Potato Chips

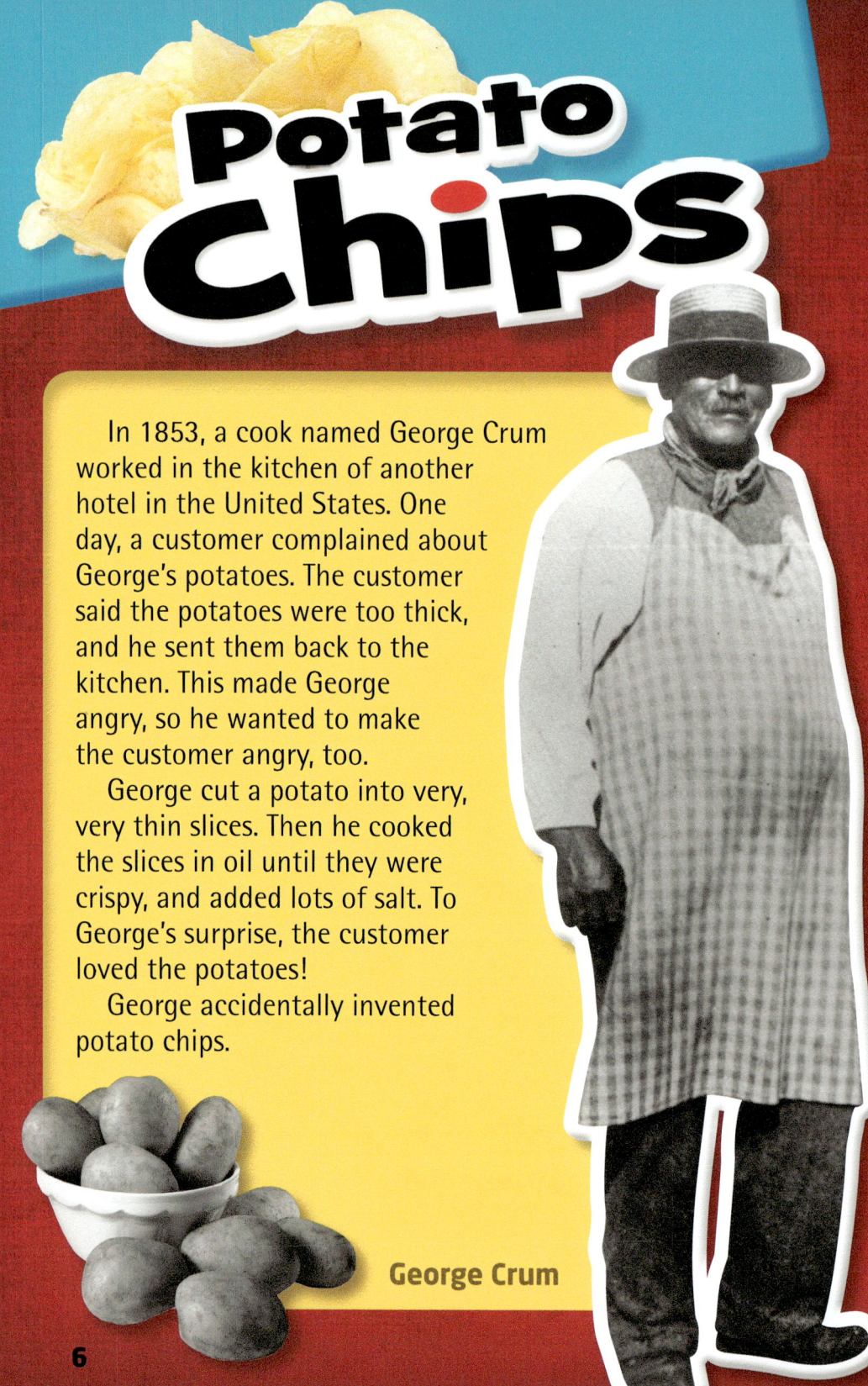

In 1853, a cook named George Crum worked in the kitchen of another hotel in the United States. One day, a customer complained about George's potatoes. The customer said the potatoes were too thick, and he sent them back to the kitchen. This made George angry, so he wanted to make the customer angry, too.

George cut a potato into very, very thin slices. Then he cooked the slices in oil until they were crispy, and added lots of salt. To George's surprise, the customer loved the potatoes!

George accidentally invented potato chips.

George Crum

Today, people around the world eat millions of pounds of potato chips each year.

Popsicles

In the early 1900s, children in the United States used to drink soda made from mixing soda water and fruit-flavored powder. One day, an eleven-year-old boy named Frank Epperson stirred his drink with a wooden stick, then left the drink outside. It was very cold that night. The next morning, Frank found his drink frozen on the stick. Frank accidentally made the first Popsicle.

Eighteen years later, Frank remembered his frozen treat. He began a business to sell it. He called the treats "Epsicles." Frank's kids called their father Pop. So they called his invention "Pop's 'sicles."

Frank Epperson

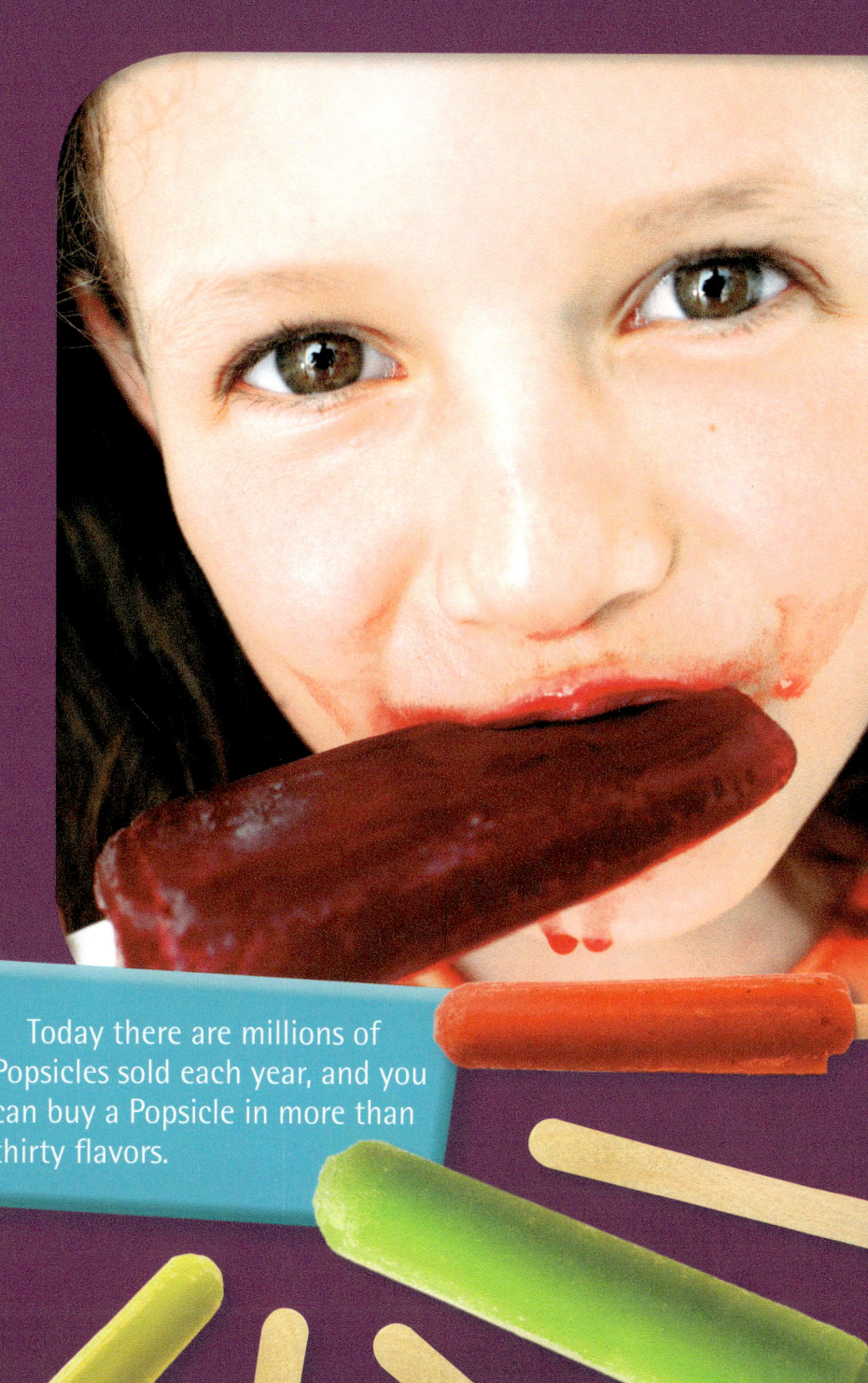

Today there are millions of Popsicles sold each year, and you can buy a Popsicle in more than thirty flavors.

Ice Cream Cones

In 1904, there was a big fair in the United States called the St. Louis World's Fair. A man named Ernest Hamwi sold thin Persian waffles at the fair. Near him, another man sold ice cream.

It was a hot summer day. People bought a lot of ice cream. Soon the ice cream seller ran out of dishes.

Ernest used his creativity to solve this problem. He rolled a waffle into a cone and put a scoop of ice cream in it. People loved it! Some think that this was the first ice cream cone.

The St. Louis World's Fair in 1904

Remember, some wonderful inventions came from accidents. You never know what an accident can lead to. So the next time you do something by accident, ask yourself: "Is there a good idea in this accident?"

Facts About Another Invention

As you've read, some popular foods were created by accident. But did you know that a popular device for cooking foods was also invented by accident?

Percy Spencer

A scientist named Percy Spencer invented the microwave oven in 1945. Percy worked with radars. Radars use radio waves to find the location of things such as boats and airplanes. During World War II, they were used to help find enemy airplanes.

One day, Percy was working with a machine that makes radio waves. Suddenly, he noticed that the candy bar in his pocket was melted. This gave him an idea. Maybe radio waves could heat food.

Percy tried another experiment. He used the radio waves on popcorn kernels. The popcorn kernels popped! He used the radio waves on an egg. The hot egg exploded all over Percy's co-worker.

By accident, Percy invented the microwave oven.

The first microwave ovens weighed 350 kilograms (about 770 pounds) and were 1.8 meters (6 feet) tall! Of course, microwave ovens are much smaller today and are used in millions of homes around the world.

A modern microwave

An early microwave

Fun with Creativity

Unscramble the words to complete the sentences.

invent   problem   solution   idea   creativity

ttiviyraec

1. This child used his ___creativity___ to make a bus out of a box.

boprmel

2. This child is trying to solve a _____.

vtneni

3. This child likes to _____ new things.

diae

4. An invention can start with a creative _____.

noostiul

5. Sometimes it is easy to find the _____ to a problem.

Draw a line from each problem to its solution.

Problem

Solution

Think of a problem you had recently. What solution did you find for this problem? Write a few sentences about the problem and your solution. Use a bilingual dictionary if necessary.

Glossary

accident something that happens in a very unusual or surprising way

crispy firm but easily broken

device a thing made to do a particular task

expected thought that something was likely to happen

fair

fair an event, usually outside, with fun activities and things to buy

frozen turned solid by very cold temperatures

guests people staying in a hotel or another person's home for a short time

melt

melt to change from a solid to a liquid usually because of heat

powder

powder a dry dust made of very small pieces

recipe a set of instructions for making a food dish

snacks food eaten between meals